I PROMISE

Reflections on Marriage

By David Martin

Dedication

To Almighty God for making the bad times bearable and the good times possible. To my devoted wife, who is my life partner, my mirror, and my muse. To my mother, who is with the Lord. I am the product of her love.

Table of Contents

Acknowledgments

This book has been eight years and six months in the making. This is how long I have been married up until the final edits. My wife, Darie Martin, has been phenomenal in her encouragement and support throughout the writing process. Her belief that I could do something I had never accomplished before comes from her faith and obedience to Jesus Christ, our Lord and Savior. I wish I could say that my own faith had been so unshakeable throughout. I would like to thank her especially for allowing me to release intimate details of our marriage so that other marriages may be encouraged, perhaps reconciled, by our testimony.

As for my children, Daniel Zachary Martin, age three, and Danaye Nicolette Martin, age one, this book is my legacy to them. Each day I look upon their beautiful faces, I remember these words do matter. Even if they are the only two who read this book, years from now, I will consider it well worth the effort. I want them to know how much I love their mother and how much I love God.

Next, I cannot overstate the importance of my pastor, Dr. A.R. Bernard, senior pastor of Christian Cultural Center in Brooklyn, New York. His teaching is the truth of God. I thank him for forcing me to confront myself these past eight years. It has been painful, at times humbling, and occasionally humorous. At all times, it has been convicting. I also thank Elder Karen Bernard, his dove, for her leadership and love. If there is any part of this book that sounds like wisdom, you can be certain it came from them.

Finally, no man is an island. I want to thank Gene and Marsha Redd, founders of the Marriage Mentoring Network. Their seven years of pouring themselves into my marriage has been God's greatest resource for my wife and I. Gene's knowledge of Scripture was invaluable to finishing this project. His consistent model of a God-fearing husband was my inspiration. They are my mentors, my joint heirs in Christ, and my dear friends.

Introduction – Fixing the Fireplace in July

I used to ask myself, "What if I did everything possible to prepare for marriage?" Would things work out differently? Would our trials be any easier? One particular marriage ministry meeting offered me some answers. Michael and Patricia Conners (fictional names), newlyweds, were giving their testimony. Though they were new to marriage, they were certainly not new to the organization, as they had attended a couple of meetings in preparation for marriage. Also part of their preparation was pre-marital counseling, dedicated prayer sessions in which they sought God's will for their future, and planning, planning, planning. In fact, Michael had come up with a spreadsheet of goals and strategies for just about every area of their marriage. They discussed the spreadsheet together and were mutually agreed, or so it appeared, over what was put on paper.

Their testimony was not about their goals and objectives as a couple. It was not about God's grand design for their marriage. They had moved into a home with a broken fireplace, and Patricia simply wanted Michael to fix it. Now the word "simply" is such a relative term, like when an advertiser describes something as affordable. Indeed, in this case, repairing a home fixture was a simple matter for someone as resourceful as Michael. But this couple would learn, as did all of us, that situations are rarely simple between a husband and wife.

Michael embodied all of the husband stereotypes: he was pragmatic, focused, task-driven, and had a struggling sensitivity when it came to the opposite sex. No surprise that when given the task of fixing the fireplace, he immediately assigned it a priority based on his usual criteria: time, resources, and urgency. They had just moved into their new home and there was no shortage of home projects to accomplish. He had precious little time since his career sent him away from home for weeks. Finally, it was the middle of July; the earliest they would use the fireplace was October.

Patricia deviated very little from the wife stereotypes: she was sensitive, traditional, and protective of the home. When she requested Michael to fix it in July, she did not mean October.

It would take me years to comprehend all of the nuances of the spiritual and social dynamics surrounding this one disagreement. But then, the reason most couples fail out of the matrimony starting gate is because they take a simple, dare I say child-like, approach to a complex matter.

Whether or not Michael learned that day about ministering to Patricia through unwavering service beyond the laws of pragmatics, I cannot say. But I did realize that day the Lord would develop in me the ability to write a book about marriage.

Marriage is God's plan that few have played out according to His blueprint. It's a higher calling to tread a narrow walkway of righteousness as imperfect beings and to be accountable to another imperfect being. It is the road our faith walks on. However, faith is only as good as the object in which it is placed. It is a lifelong practice that requires exacting discipline and self-control.

Yet for all the challenges facing couples, Christians, non-Christians, and even atheists get married everyday. Many people marry more than once. Obviously there must be some benefit to marriage that we desperately want. It's like sticking a key through a wall of flame to unlock the door on the other side and obtain the prize that will make the pain worthwhile. That prize is God's purpose for our life through our marriage. Yet most marriages fail before ever discovering that purpose. At best, a couple may manage to endure the trials of marriage and even have marginally productive lives that could have been achieved apart. At worst, they could waste precious years in torment and have children who perpetuate the cycle before finally allowing their marriage to end in divorce.

Faith is only as good as the object in which it is placed.

There are three universal purposes for all marriages. The first is achieving oneness and reflecting the image of God. The second is so that man may have a helpmate in his spiritual walk. The third is to multiply a godly legacy. Compelling as these purposes are, can they motivate couples to stay together through the tough times? I am referring to truly tough times that cause a person to consider if he or she made the right decision in life. Perhaps so, but recent trends indicate they have not been enough.

Three universal purposes for marriage

- Achieve oneness
- Have a helpmate
- Multiply a godly legacy

A marriage needs to find its unique purpose beyond these commonalities. It needs to be spiritually arranged by God so it impacts the greater society and brings glory to His kingdom.

At the time of writing this, I have been married to my wife, Darie, for eight years. We have two children. Some say we have not been together long enough to have experienced what marriage is all about. I don't know if they are right. I do know that in eight years, we have experienced regret, strife, death, unfaithfulness, and sickness. The illusion of marital bliss wore off very quickly after the wedding, and we were both left wondering what we got into.

It did not help that my single life was hardly a model of obedient Christian living. I am sure those who knew me best placed bets on just how long this marriage would last. My life of self-indulgence and reckless promiscuity along with virtually no preparation emotionally, financially, or spiritually made us a divorce statistic waiting to happen.

God says in Jeremiah 29:11–14,

> "For I know the plans I have for you," declares the LORD, "plans to prosper you and not to harm you, plans to give you hope and a future. Then you will call upon me and come and pray to me, and I will listen to you. You will seek me and find me when you seek me with all your heart. I will be found by you," declares the LORD, "and will bring you back from captivity. I will gather you from all the nations and places where I have banished you," declares the LORD, "and will bring you back to the place from which I carried you into exile."

All He needs is a willing heart, an open mind, and a penitent spirit. I did not want to divorce my wife, nor did I want to be miserable for the rest of my life. I had nowhere to turn but to God. He seized upon that opportunity to rescue me from my captivity and deliver me from my banishment back to His waiting arms.

Through all of our difficulties, I found a purpose for my life, for our marriage. Most importantly, I have a personal relationship with my Creator, God, which did not exist when I was single. I was once filled with regret; now I would not trade the first eight years for all the pleasure in the world.

Perhaps marriage prepares us for our purpose as well as provides us with a companion. My pastor preaches that in using our individual talents, we live life on levels and experience it in stages. All the while we must submit ourselves so God can strengthen our character at each stage. We experience new stages in our marriage over the years. If your character is not strong enough to deal with the new responsibility and authority God has placed upon you, you may put asunder what God has ordained.

A successful marriage should grow from being a basic social unit of a man and woman in an interdependent relationship to one that eventually impacts a society at large. Your marriage should become a reason why people should get married, not a reason why not. There is no social institution on Earth that is more rewarding, fulfilling, or powerful than a successful marriage. On the other hand, there is no worse situation to be in than a failed marriage. I don't advocate two miserable people staying together merely for the sake of the children. Two miserable people should stop blaming their spouse and take responsibility for their own misery. Let God work it out because no one can steal the joy of Christ from us; we can only choose to give it away.

It is my sincere prayer you read this book with an eye on your marriage. It is one clueless man's chronicle of his start on a magnificent journey. I tried to be as transparent as I could. The Word says no man is tested except by what is common to all men. The theme of this book is you are not alone in your trials. However, your marriage is God's doing. Your ultimate purpose is for His glory. Fix the broken fireplaces in your relationship. It's the key to your happiness!

Be inspired by my journey.

Letter to Darie

He who finds a wife finds what is good and receives favor from the LORD.

Proverbs 18:22

Dear Darie,

Within these pages, I chronicle my thoughts. I will try to be as honest and transparent as possible. With God's help, you will come to know me more intimately: my thoughts, fears, regrets, hopes, dreams, fascinations, and denials. May God guide my hand so my words are clear and what is in my heart is made known. I can think of no better gift to you. That we were meant to spend to the rest of our days together is a prelude to heaven.

Back in 1999, marriage was so new to me. All I knew was I wanted to be married to you, but I wasn't quite sure how. I just sensed we went as far as we were going to go dating. I wanted something different. My relationship with you had to stand out from all that came before. You were special, and I did not want to treat this relationship like any other.

I did not know the Lord before we were married. I thrived in the world, and my morals were easily compromised. This made my decision to get married so much harder. In the back of my mind, I knew I would eventually lose you unless I changed my life forever.

The days leading up to my proposal were some of the most frightening of my life. What would marriage be like? Could I ever be faithful when I never was? Was I doing this for the right reasons? Would you say yes? Many questions, and yet I never once asked God. But God was at work anyway. How faithful is the Lord we serve.

Had I listened to Him, I would have heard Him say, "My son, it is time to put childish things away. You have been disobedient and self-serving all your life. Now you are out of people or circumstances to blame. You cannot claim ignorance for I have revealed myself to you many times. As penance, your journey will be that much more hampered by fear and doubt. You will lament, mourn, and weep because your eyes only see the sin you hold so dear yet must repent of. But I am the Lord your God, and I know the plans I have for you, plans to prosper you and not harm you, plans to give you a hope and a future."

Had I listened, I would have realized marriage would not be easy because I had sinned against the Lord. In His infinite love, He saw fit to give me you as a precious gift anyway. I ask you to forgive me, sweetheart, as I ask the Lord for forgiveness. I had blinders on and I could not see. Now I am out of excuses. You are God's plan for me, my hope and my future.

Scripture References

1 Corinthians 13:11

Discussion Questions

What childish things did you have to put away when
you got married?

What childish things still creep into your relationship?

What issues from your past are making marriage
difficult?

Staking Your Reputation

But the LORD said to Samuel, "Do not consider his appearance or his height, for I have rejected him. The LORD does not look at the things man looks at. Man looks at the outward appearance, but the LORD looks at the heart."

1 Samuel 16:7

If someone says something about you and another agrees, you have a reputation. This is your outward appearance, consisting partly of rumor, largely of conjecture, mostly of assumptions, and a little bit of observation. What you do in private reveals your true character, the heart of a man.

Too often in marriage, we marry a reputation. Reputation speaks to your public performance. However, marriage reveals a person's character. What God sees when no one is around is what a spouse soon sees. When two people date for years only to divorce soon after a wedding, they married a reputation only to soon discover their spouse's true character.

Reputation speaks to your public performance. However, marriage reveals a person's character.

When Darie and I first met, we were both committed full-time to multi-level marketing (MLM), also known as network marketing. For those unfamiliar with MLMs, let me just say it is all about appearance. A person's reputation is critical to achieving success in this arena, so I diligently guarded mine.

I often presented to crowds of one hundred or more, so I was always well-dressed, groomed, and polished. No matter what I was going through in private, my manner was cheerful, positive, and encouraging to others. The jargons of network marketers consist of success buzz words like "opportunity," "fantastic," "awesome," "making money," and "exploding."

Darie and I met after one of my presentations. I don't remember my first words, but my standard introduction would go something like this: "Hi, it's great to meet you. This is a fantastic business, but it is not for everyone. Do you see an opportunity for yourself? Awesome. Your sister brought you here? She is new herself and already building a successful business in the New York area. If you want to make money, stick with her, get all the training you can, and watch your business explode!"

Does this sound like a sappy salesperson speech? You would be amazed how effective it could be when your reputation precedes you. Darie had no doubt been informed beforehand that I was one of the top leaders in the area who was rapidly building a huge organization and knew just about everything it took to prosper in this business. When she finally met me, all I had to do was maintain a consistent appearance long enough to seal the deal. Four years later, we did just that at the altar.

Where carnal motivations such as pride and wealth motivate us to maintain an appealing reputation, a person's character is inherently flawed. Herein lies the first great problem with marriage. Human beings are trained to notice flaws, a tendency stifled only by intense levels of romantic feelings, as in the courting stage of a relationship. While the public has the pleasure of dealing with your spouse's reputation, you wake up every day to the nasty, imperfect, unattractive, annoying, and sometimes distressing character flaws.

One year into marriage, neither of us were doing network marketing. I was no longer the figure of striking success she saw in the front of the room. Instead, I was this uncertain, struggling, at times fearful husband who was reluctant to take charge of our new life together.

Now here are the rules of the game. You cannot change, manipulate, or in any way directly control your spouse. However, you do have the complete ability, not to mention responsibility, to work on your character. As your first act of improvement, train yourself to stop looking at the character flaws of your spouse. The second act is much more difficult. We must lay down our pride and work on the character flaws our spouse sees in us.

Most people won't do that because it requires them to change some of their private practices, their habits, and their disciplines. The self resists such a notion. "Why should I have to give up something that has served me so well?"

Deep down, no one wants to undergo the humbling experience of improving their character. Yet Jesus, who is to all Christians the model of a perfect man, humbled Himself before God. Philippians 2:5-11 reads,

> Your attitude should be the same as that of Christ Jesus: Who, being in very nature God, did not consider equality with God something to be grasped, but made himself nothing, taking the very nature of a servant, being made in human likeness. And being found in appearance as a man, he humbled himself. Therefore God exalted him to the highest place and gave him the name that is above every name, that at the name of Jesus every knee should bow, in heaven and on earth and under the earth, and every tongue confess that Jesus Christ is Lord, to the glory of God the Father.

Change for God, yes, but for my spouse? Someone who is flawed, uncertain, fearful, unreasonable? The self, who desires to be lord, views this notion as preposterous.

I knew my wife was disappointed in my early performance as a husband. Looking back, I cannot blame her. However, I did blame her. Up until marriage, my reputation had served me quite well. Along came my wife to point out all my secret flaws without even saying a word. It was infuriating and it was humbling, but it was true. The truth was that in the business, I had a reputation of success, but because of certain flaws in my character, I did not achieve success.

Though Jesus was perfect, He sacrificed His reputation. He died a humiliating death, allowing others to think He was a false prophet and a blasphemer when He was in fact the Son of God. He was a man with no flaws who suffered for the flaws others saw in Him. Because of that one act, God looks past all of our flaws. It reads in 2 Corinthians 5:21, "God made him who had no sin to be sin for us, so that in him we might become the righteousness of God."

You say you want to be like Jesus? What are you willing to sacrifice for the flaws your spouse sees in you? Starting today, stop defending your reputation and start building your character.

Scripture References

1 Samuel 16:7
Philippians 2:5 – 11
2 Corinthians 5:21
2 Corinthians 10:7
1 Peter 3:3-4

Discussion Questions

What was your spouse's reputation when you married?
What have you discovered about your spouse's character since you have been married?
What areas of your character did you have to improve since you have been married?

My Song

What has God ordained
To bring you so near perfection?
Oh, mirror to my soul
I am unworthy of your reflection.

Falling in Love is easy.
Choosing to love is divine.
If I loved you less I would still love you more
Than all the world's beauty combined.

Your body, a gift
To unwrap everyday of the year.
Your caress soothes my aching soul,
The crystal on my stairs

Your face so exquisite
With eyes all aglow.
Your beauty like Christmas time
In the fresh fallen snow.

A feast for my senses.
A challenge to my restrain.
Oh, the possibilities
our romance contains!

Come to me my Love.
I await you in the twilight hour.
Sing to me with your kisses.
Sensuous is your power.

I have prepared our bed chamber
With scents and sounds to delight.
God has ordained you and I together
To be holy in his sight.

Scripture References

Song of Songs

Discussion Questions

What is your song to your spouse?

Lost Inheritance

I have learned to hear You in the early dawn, a time of perpetual new beginning, when the entire world is reset. You have my full attention. I will eventually crowd You out in favor of the pressing circumstances of the day. But in the early dawn, there is no fear, anxiety, disappointment, or strife. All those things are in the day to come, as in the day before.

In the early dawn, my mind is as still as a meadow without a breeze. I can hear You whispering to my spirit, hurriedly, urgently, as my little son does when I walk through the door after a long workday. Like him, You know You have precious little time to speak with me before something draws me away.

You whisper truth into my life. The truth of who I am and my purpose for being here. You say how much You love me and I don't have to remain in my state of confusion, frustration, or worry. All I have to do is trust You and follow in the steps You laid out for me and I can live life more abundantly. My wife would be happier; my children would have everything they need. I would find fulfillment in my purpose, which is…

The phone rings, the children awake, and the clock chimes. It's time for work, and the early dawn is over, soon to be followed by the concerns of the day. Your voice, Lord, is drowned in a sea of tasks on an endless to-do list.

When decades have passed, I suspect those interludes of dawn will get longer and longer as those concerns that so occupied my time disappear with my youth. You won't have to speak to me in such a hurried and urgent manner anymore, Lord. I suspect Your voice will be tempered with consoling and lament. With fewer days to come, the early dawn will soon be all that is left. I will have an eternity to hear all I could have become.

I was thirty-seven when I heard the call to serve the Lord. By then I had amassed enough excuses why not to serve Him. I was married with two small children and a struggling consulting business, and I was chin deep in debt. It was all I could do to pay the bills and tend to my family every month. I thought if I began spreading the gospel, I would be spreading myself too thin.

I was not a complete stranger to ministry. Darie and I were members of a marriage support network for five years and went on to join a marriage ministry at our church. No one questioned our commitment. But commitment to me means you take steps that cannot be undone. I have noticed people who are "committed" to ministry and work a full-time job. Something valuable always suffers that cannot be undone.

**Commitment is when you take steps that cannot
be undone.**

Thousands of years ago, Abraham was promised
descendents as numerous as the stars in the sky, and still
he slept with his wife's servant. Abraham took steps
that could not be undone. He made the mistake most
people who hear God's call do; he focused on what he
didn't have, a fertile wife, instead of what he had. The
fruit of that unfaithful act was the people of Ishmael,
whose descendents became a great nation. But impres-
sive as it was, Isaac's descendents were Abraham's
inheritance and the world's salvation. Thousands of
years later, the world still pays the price for Ishmael.

**Abraham made the mistake most people who hear
God's call do; he focused on what he didn't have
instead of what he had.**

God's great promise is still kept. My inheritance
lies before me as a child of God adopted into His
family of twelve tribes. I have been shown as much in
my ministry. Yet like Abraham, I stubbornly choose to
go my own way, led by false prophets and sinful pride,
afraid to take steps I cannot undo. Those whom God
called, He also equipped, but I cannot see the promise
beyond my lack. My family suffers my Ishmael. Who
knows how many others will also suffer because I
settled for Ishmael when God promised me Isaac?

Scripture References

Genesis 15:4-5
Genesis 16
2 Peter 1:3-4

Discussion Questions

Do you know what God has promised you?
Do you know what God has called you to do?
What steps have you taken to demonstrate your faith
    in His call?
What have you ever settled for that was not God's
    best for you?

Marriage Dance

When a couple dances well together, as in a tango, waltz, or mambo, it is very symbolic of oneness in a relationship. To begin with, the man leads with gentle yet direct prompting. The woman responds in the direction she is guided yet incorporates her own flare into the spins, gestures, and footwork. The man is confident, so he does not even think about the steps. He is guided by an unseen force that dictates each move before he does it. With each turn, lift, and dip, the couple inevitably returns to the basics of the routine. They maintain eye contact, their posture is perfect, and their movement is in total harmony, otherwise the dance would not be good. The woman completely trusts her partner won't mishandle, disrespect, or damage her body in any way. Most importantly, the couple is always on beat to the music. Anyone watching the couple long enough could eventually learn the dance as well, so consistent are they with their motions.

This is God's divine design for marriage! The man is the spiritual leader of the marriage dance. His leadership is gentle yet direct, in accordance with his role as a tender warrior. The woman is commanded to submit to her husband, yet this does not mean subservience, for her own identity influences every step. The husband demonstrates confidence and courage in the direction his family is headed because God Almighty controls his decisions. The turns, lifts, and dips are the struggles in the relationship. It takes trust, harmony, and practice to execute difficult routines in a dance or overcome difficult times in a marriage. Just remember, with each struggle you overcome, the dance becomes more beautiful.

As long as the couple maintains the foundation of their faith, the marriage dance continues. The success of the marriage is based on how well each partner executes the role as husband and wife and maintains a relationship built on trust. They must dance to God's music at all times. Done well, they will shine the light of God into the world for others to follow.

Wikipedia defines *oneness* as a spiritual term referring to the "experience" of the absence of ego identity boundaries and, according to some traditions, the perception of an absolute interconnectedness of all matter and thought in space-time, or one's ultimate identity with God. Oneness is unique to a Christian marriage because we are the only ones who identify with a resurrected Lord and Savior. Unlike alternative lifestyles, Christians have an eternal model in Jesus Christ, who we can emulate in our quest to identify with God. To the degree that a couple identifies with Jesus, the two are on the path to becoming one in Christ.

Oneness is unique to a Christian marriage because we are the only ones who identify with a resurrected Lord and Savior.

In John 17:20 – 23, Christ prayed,

My prayer is not for them alone. I pray also for those who will believe in me through their message, that all of them may be one, Father, just as you are in me and I am in you. May they also be in us so that the world may believe that you have sent me. I have given them the glory that you gave me, that they may be one as we are one: I in them and you in me. May they be brought to complete unity to let the world know that you sent me and have loved them even as you have loved me.

The message of a married couple is oneness and a unity in Christ so the world may believe. How can we unify as a church body if a husband and wife, the most basic social unit, cannot unite?

If you are experiencing marital difficulties, ask yourself the following question: "What do I believe about this marriage?" Is it for your convenience, your carnal fulfillment, to make you happy? If this is so, then you should plan to live in spiritual separation with stressful times ahead because there can be no happiness in marriage without compromise. Is it the vehicle in which you are allowing Jesus to restore you to the image of God and make the world believe? You are still going to have challenges to your relationship because you are not as Christ-like as you may think. The difference is your trials are toward a positive result. Count it all as joy.

Scripture References

Genesis 2: 24
Mark 10: 42-43
1 Corinthians 11: 11

Discussion Questions

In what areas of you marriage do you show complete
    unity and agreement?
In what areas is there a lack of unity?

The Dollhouse

Kate's dollhouse had everything a girl could want. Three floors, several guest rooms, a large kitchen with a nook, lavish furnishings, and a pretty Chevy Malibu parked in the garage. But her home and career did not make Kate happy. She felt it was lacking one major thing: a man to fill it.

One day while shopping in the mall with her girl-friends, she saw him. He was perched high up on a shelf, clean cut, anatomically correct, and had what seemed to Kate a picture perfect smile. She had to take him home.

All of Kate's girlfriends congratulated her on such a lucky find. Kate just knew some were bitterly jealous. Things were terrific for a while. They lived in her dollhouse with many rooms, took long trips in Kate's Malibu sports car, and had fabulous tea parties with her other friends.

But each morning as Kate left for work, leaving behind Ken's smiling face at the kitchen table, it bothered her just a little more. At the end of the day, Kate would come home eager to talk about her day or just have pleasant conversation. However, Ken never had anything to say. He would just sit there staring back at her with that same annoying smile. It wasn't long before Kate came up with a mental list of other grievances. For starters, he had no income. He did not help keep the dollhouse neat. She always had to initiate dates, and it felt to Kate like he just didn't care.

One day Kate received the shock of her life after a brief bout of morning sickness and a quick home test. Now they had to make this work, she thought. She was about to have the family she always wanted. Nine months later, little Catalina was born.

For Ken's part, he tried oh so desperately to live up to these new expectations. He applied for jobs, but he never had the right accessories, or he did not have enough digits on his hands, or he just wasn't as flexible as the latest action figures. Ken would come home dejected and go riding in the Malibu for hours, flirting with other dolls. When Kate came home, he had nothing good to say, so he just sat in the kitchen holding his plastic cup and staring out the window with the lace curtains.

With a steel resolve and a heart as plastic as Ken's, Kate decided to go it on her own. She put her dollhouse in the attic and moved out with Catalina. It was not long before the emptiness returned. She attempted to fill it with man after man, and each time her standards grew less idealistic. She no longer had time to play house. She had bills to pay, and child-care was expensive.

As for Ken, he went from girl to girl, never truly feeling at home. His occasional visits with Catalina were all he looked forward to. He was eventually shelved forever, obsolete and neglected.

Time passed and little Catalina grew up and moved into a dollhouse of her own. Its rooms were empty, her heart was lonely, and she went perusing the malls. There on a shelf, tall and handsome, impeccably dressed, was a Ken staring back at her with a perfect smile.

The second commandment in Exodus 20:4-6 says,

> You shall not make for yourself an idol in the form of anything in heaven above or on the earth beneath or in the waters below. You shall not bow down to them or worship them; for I, the Lord your God, am a jealous God, punishing the children for the sin of the fathers to the third and fourth generation of those who hate me, but showing love to a thousand {generations} of those who love me and keep my commandments.

When a little child plays with a dollhouse, it's an imaginary game. When an adult plays with a doll-house, it's an ephod of lies and counterfeit. Families don't have enough money to tithe faithfully because they have none left over after the mortgage and the car payments. Couples have no time to serve each other or God because of their demanding careers. Television programs and sports events are given more consistent attention than Bible study.

When a little child plays with a dollhouse, it's an imaginary game. When an adult plays with a dollhouse, it's an ephod of lies and counterfeit.

Our home, lifestyle, and even our spouse can become idols we worship. Predictably, when they fail to meet our needs, we try to put them on the shelf like a doll. The problem is we cannot put our marriages on a shelf when things don't work out. A marriage doesn't just collect dust. It collects memories and a legacy of broken homes and single parent drudgery.

The wrong motivation for getting married is not an excuse to get out. Thankfully, Romans 8:28 tells us that God works for the good of those who love Him, who have been called according to His purpose. Our bad decisions will not mess up God's master plan. He has already worked it out.

The wrong motivation for getting married is not an excuse to get out.

One of the three universal purposes for marriage is to multiply a godly legacy. Genesis 1:28a reads, "God said to them, 'Be fruitful and multiply and fill the earth.'" Modern times would seem to suggest we don't need marriage to accomplish this. Single parent statistics are astonishing. Television programs bombard us with all types of family arrangements.

As ambassadors of God's kingdom, the married couple must provide the divine context for having children. Neither women nor men are made emotionally, spiritually, or physically to raise children by themselves. Child rearing requires a team effort. A daughter must see how her daddy loves and respects her mommy on a consistent basis. A son must see his father take responsibility as the head of the household, solving problems and keeping the family together through tough times. There must be adequate income to the household to support all the children's needs without needing to work multiple jobs that take you away from your most important job of all.

Ask yourself the following question: What do you believe about your marriage? If you don't like the answer, then make a change starting today. The fate of your children and their children down to the third and fourth generation may hinge on the next decision you make.

Scripture References

Genesis 1:28
Exodus 20:4-6

Discussion Questions

What has become or is in danger of becoming an idol in your life?

What do you practice consistently to demonstrate God's preeminence in your life?

What habits do you have that you would rather not see your children emulate?

Prenuptials

The groom looked at his watch before opening the door to the arbitration room. He was very late. He thought briefly of providing an excuse, but somehow losing his bowtie and having to pick up another from the tuxedo store seemed too lame a defense. He opened the door, and there at the oval mahogany table sat his beautiful bride in full regalia.

She looked over at him and smiled. The groom smiled back; no excuse was necessary. Also seated at what passed for the head of the table was the world, a big blue and green ball. It was to be the arbitrator at these proceedings. The world looked over at him and grinned, saying, "Take a seat, you're right on time." The groom took a seat directly across from his bride.

The world began by saying, "As you Christians do not believe in prenuptials, we will not call it that. Consider this an arrangement between two consenting parties that will provide some assurances in case of irreconcilable differences." The bride and groom looked at each other and nodded their agreement. The world grinned. "Shall we begin with a word of prayer?"

Article 1 – Failed Expectations

Should the groom fail to meet the expectations of the bride, as put forth in Addendum A: Conditions of the Bride, the bride shall in no way be obligated to perform any of the marital duties specified in the Holy Bible and may do so at her sole discretion.

Article 2 – Disability

In the event that either party is rendered incapable of performing in his or her role either due to physical or mental impediment, the other withholds the option to procure similar services from outside the marriage union without explicit consent of the disabled partner. The duration and scope of these services is determined by the procurer, who is under no obligation to cease this course of action should the marital partner return to full functioning status.

Article 3 – Infidelity

Should either party engage in any act of sexual impurity, including but not limited to viewing pornography, masturbation, or lasciviousness, the offended partner has the right to invoke the penalty of divorce on the grounds of self-righteousness.

Article 4 – Financial Ramifications

Should the husband fail to financially support the wife in a manner to which she is accustomed, as put forth in Addendum B: lifestyle expectations, the wife may choose to terminate the marriage or procure a separate income stream for her personal use.

Article 5 – Withholding Intimacy

If at any time either party experiences disappointment, regret, or general dissatisfaction with the marriage, that party reserves the right to withhold affection or to disengage in any form of intimate behavior with the spouse until such time as he or she feels better about the specific situation.

Article 6 – Obedience to God

Both spouses are to exercise strict obedience to God Almighty to the extent that it does not make either party uncomfortable or cause them to relinquish in any way deeply held convictions about sex, finances, and relationships.

The world concluded by saying, "Now if there is no further business to discuss, I ask that you each prick your finger and trace your signatures at the bottom of this document with your blood, and it will be binding." The world exacted its fee and merrily went on its way. The couple left hand in hand to the chapel to begin a life of wedded bliss with the assurance that their personal interests were protected.

And Jesus wept.

Scripture References

1 Corinthians 13:8-13
1 Corinthians 11:11
Galatians 3:28
Ephesians 5:23
Ephesians 5:28-30
1 Timothy 5:8
Malachi 2:14-15

Discussion Questions

What mental prenuptials did you come into the marriage with?

In what areas have you died to self for the sake of the relationship?

What are some worldly perspectives on marriage that are destructive to your marriage?

Husband, Leader, Visionary

You cannot speak about visionary leadership from a biblical perspective without referencing the life of Moses. He exhibited all the traits of a good leader, which is no surprise since he had a lot of preparation through his experiences and education.

I have held leadership roles in school and business, but by far, my most enduring role has been as a husband. In this role, I had no experience or education. I believe the head of the family was intended to be a man's first leadership responsibility. Dr. Miles Munroe, pastor of Bahamas Faith Ministries International, said, "A man's ministry is as strong as his bedroom." A great husband is a visionary leader. A visionary leader is one who motivates others toward achieving a shared purpose by modeling the values, behaviors, and discipline necessary to achieve it.

A vision is a clear, specific description of a purpose, sometimes using symbols or metaphors. For example, Moses' purpose was to free the Israelites from Egyptian bondage. The vision was to lead his people to the Promised Land, a land flowing with milk and honey.

Painting the vision falls on the shoulders of the leader. If a wife is called to submit to her husband, then he had better be describing a picture of something that's worth the sacrifice. If a woman pledges herself to a man with no vision, she will eventually reclaim her independence.

Your marriage needs to have a purpose that is given a higher priority over any trial it goes through. That purpose should be described in a vision. In order for this vision to take hold in the marriage, it must be both extrinsic and intrinsic.

> **If a woman pledges herself to a man with no vision, she will eventually reclaim her independence.**

Extrinsic vision means focusing on something relative to a competitor. It is limited to defeating an opponent. Once achieved, it becomes a defensive posture. Examples of extrinsic visions are marrying for money, marrying because of pregnancy, or marrying because of fear of loss. Some women marry a man because they think he will be a good provider and will meet their need for security. Some men marry because they don't want to be the last one of their buddies to get married and they are feeling a little peer pressure. Once an extrinsic vision is achieved, it no longer motivates the person to sustain the relationship. The other spouse is now put in a position to defend the decision to get married in the first place.

In the case of the Israelites, the competitors were Pharaoh and Egypt. The extrinsic vision was escaping slavery. Their competitor appeared to be defeated after the parting of the Red Sea. Moses' vision of the Promised Land became less motivating once the heat was off. With the extrinsic vision achieved, the idea of wandering in the desert homeless was not so appealing. As a matter of fact, only two months into their journey, bondage to Egypt was beginning to become preferable. Moses found himself defending his position and narrowly avoided getting stoned on two occasions.

Once an extrinsic vision is achieved, it no longer motivates the person to sustain the relationship.

A husband often makes the mistake of creating extrinsic visions only. For instance, he may demonstrate how well he can take care of his wife financially. At first, the wife may seem very excited and in agreement. But later, she decides she is unwilling to pay the high price for financial security. Perhaps the husband has to work long hours and weekends. She may seem to turn against the visionary who must now defend the reason why he works so hard. This is because the vision was only extrinsic to her. A similar scenario can exist in any area: communication, sex, children, etc... For a vision to have a lasting influence, it must also become intrinsic.

Intrinsic vision is creating a new product, taking an old product to a new level, or setting a new standard. God did all three of these things in order to instill an intrinsic vision in His people. Numbers 14:20-25 describes how He created a new product in the next generation of Israelites after forty years of wandering. Numbers 1 and 3-5 describes how He took an old product to a new level with organizing this new generation into a fighting army. Exodus 20 and the book of Leviticus describe how He created a new standard with His laws handed down through Moses.

A husband must also do these things to intrinsically motivate his wife. He needs to create a new product in order to instill the vision, which is the idea of becoming one in marriage. He must take an old product to a new level, working on himself and his original vision if he had one before marriage. He must set new standards in order to model what it will take to achieve that vision. Working seven days a week may be possible for a single person, but it is a major hindrance to building intimacy in a marriage.

A husband must set new standards in order to model what it will take to achieve the vision.

Visionary leadership is more about motivating people than providing them with directions. A husband must graphically and clearly depict where a marriage is headed and why. He must make the vision both extrinsic and intrinsic if he is to have any lasting motivation on his wife. A vision is not imparted merely by writing a statement and sticking it to the wall. It must exist in the heart and mind of a leader and be lived even before it comes to fruition. Finally, any vision must be flexible enough to adapt to change according to God's will and purposes.

Jeremiah 29:11 reads, "'For I know the plans I have for you,' declares the LORD, 'plans to prosper you and not to harm you, plans to give you hope and a future.'"

Scripture References

Numbers 1, 3-5
Numbers 14:20-25
Exodus 20
Book of Leviticus

Discussion Questions

What is the vision that is set for your family?
Are you and your spouse in complete agreement with
    that vision and the method to achieve it?
What are some extrinsic visions that have already
    been achieved in your marriage?

Call Me Achan

"But the Israelites acted unfaithfully in regard to the devoted things; Achan son of Carmi, the son of Zimri, the son of Zerah, of the tribe of Judah, took some of them. So the LORD's anger burned against Israel."

Joshua 7:1

Jericho was a great walled city near the Jordan River in the land of Canaan. The Israelites, under Joshua's command, marched around the city and with a trumpet blast and a shout, God collapsed the walls down around its citizens. Yet the easy victory came with a provision. All the plunder, the silver and gold and bronze and iron were sacred to the Lord and were to go into his treasury. Yet Achan disobeyed and took two hundred shekels of silver, a wedge of gold, and a robe from Babylonia and hid them in his tent.

The story of Achan is about one man's sin, yet it begins, "But the Israelites acted unfaithfully..." Sin has consequences on all who are close to it. Christ paid the ultimate consequence for our sins because He was close to us. My wife pays the consequences for my sins because she is close to me.

Sin has consequences on all who are close to it.

Every person has pulled an Achan at one time or another—coveting worldly pleasures we were supposed to give up to God. Sometimes we fool ourselves into thinking we gave it up and even pray to God to help us in our "weakness." The truth is we bury it in our tent where no one knows.

Before I was married, my Achan manifested in promiscuous behavior. After I married, it became more covert. The Internet and magazine catalogues offered ample opportunity to indulge in secret. But the real article of silver and gold in my tent was cable television. I had purchased an unauthorized cable box from a friend which gave me access to all the channels that were not on my plan, including "adult" channels. At first, I would browse past the channels rather quickly, never lingering. After all, I was a Christian. Gradually, however, when my wife was not home, I would watch them more often. Soon I began to wait until she was asleep and sneak into the living room late at night. It was not long before it became a nightly ritual.

I prayed to God to deliver me from the temptation that led to vivid fantasies and frequent masturbation. All the while, my cable box gave me all the access I craved, hidden away in my tent. Yet how could I expect the Lord to deliver me from bondage when I held fast to the chains?

Joshua 7:13 reads, "That which is devoted is among you, O Israel. You cannot stand against your enemies until you remove it." God was not being mean and selfish to the Israelites by commanding that all the precious materials be devoted to Him. He had things for them that were much more precious than silver, gold, and bronze. They had a whole promised land to claim for God's sake! Moses told them as much before he died (Deuteronomy 28:1-14).

We must obey God in order to come into the fullness of the blessings He has for us. Today, we don't have a Joshua or a Moses to give us daily instructions: go here, stop there, take that city, or be consecrated. We do have Jesus Christ, and though He has not yet returned in person, He still gives us our daily commands in a still, small voice. At least that is how I hear God, almost at the horizon of my consciousness. I had to learn to recognize it was coming from Him and not from me.

As punishment for Achan's disobedience, the Israelites suffered a humiliating defeat in their battle against the city of Ai. I am sure Achan had opportunity to repent of his sin privately. He probably appealed to God for forgiveness even while he had the stolen items. I also had the chance to repent, but my cable box remained hooked up. I had the chance for God to deal with me privately.

After they lost the battle, Achan should have definitely come clean, but by then it was probably too late. I emphasize with Achan, agonizing every day over the sin he committed. He could not sell the metals, nor could he make it into jewelry. The Israelites could not wear jewelry after that golden calf debacle. Also, he would look pretty conspicuous wearing a thick new robe among his tribe. All the while, perhaps there was a still, soft voice telling him to give up the plunder.

Achan may have dismissed the notion as an extreme desperate thought of his own, but it was God's voice telling him what he needed to do to be free. I prayed fervently for deliverance from pornography. I found myself on my knees at the altar of my church. All the while, I ignored that crazy notion to give up my cable box. Give up free HBO? I wanted deliverance, but let's not get extreme! I dismissed the voice as my own desperate notion. The truth was God was trying to deal with me privately. I wouldn't listen; instead I prayed.

Achan did not listen either, so God had Joshua deal with him publicly. Tribe by tribe, man by man, each was paraded in front of Joshua until the culprit who caused their defeat was discerned. Could you imagine what Achan was thinking while he waited his turn among thousands? The punishment for such a crime was death by stoning—not just the perpetrator, but the entire family! Achan must have known he was headed toward his death, and he condemned his family to the same fate all because he chose not to listen to that still, small voice and give up the source of his inequity.

Eventually, I did listen, but not before the passion in my marriage had suffered. My career also suffered from all the hours of staying up late and not being able to perform on the job. At first I merely disconnected the cable box but left it in place. When you flee from temptation, you have to close off all avenues to return or you will find your way back. I would simply reconnect the box and backslide all over again. At last, I discarded the box permanently.

That evening, my poor wife sat down to watch her favorite HBO program and wondered why there was only an "unauthorized" message on the screen. She looked at me, perplexed. I only told her I disconnected the box for good. She shrugged her shoulders and turned to another channel. Eventually I explained the whole situation to my wife. She shared with me that she had been feeling rejected and undesirable to me and began to withdraw emotionally. As beautiful as she was, there was no competing with TV fantasies that catered to my sinful nature. There was a growing separation between us just two years into marriage. We were reaping the harvest of my disobedience. Unlike Achan, I gave up the plunder and, together with my wife, went before the Lord to repent and rededicate our relationship to His will and purposes. We vowed to work together to restore the passion and intimacy that had suffered for so long and threatened to destroy our fledgling marriage. The truth had set me free.

When you flee from temptation, you have to close off all avenues to return or you will find your way back.

I still deal with sexual temptation in my mind. It is every man's battle. All the while there is the still, small voice of God telling me everything is going to be okay. He has something better for me in my promised land. But it was too late to deal with me privately. Like Achan, God dealt with me publicly—not by law, but by love. First I confessed it to my wife, and then eventually to my Christian brothers and sisters so that my testimony might be a blessing to others who were facing similar struggles and ignoring the still, small voice saying to them, "If you want to be free, let go of the chains."

Scripture References

Joshua 7
Deuteronomy 28: 1-14

Discussion Questions

What objects of affection are you hiding in your tent
that hinders the full blessings of God in your
life?
Are you holding on to any objects of affection that
have no relevance to your marriage?

Tears of the Past

Into everyone's life
A little rain must fall.
But if you should look at
Each tear upon each sullen face,
You will find it reflects
Some bitter memory,
Some regretful moment,
Perhaps a missed opportunity
Or lost hope.
Let them fall
One after another
Sadness, despair, anguish
They can only exist in the past.

Scripture References

Esther 9: 22
Psalm 90: 10
Psalm 116: 8-9
Isaiah 35: 10
Isaiah 60: 20

Discussion Questions

What regrets, sorrows, or bitter memories are you
   holding on to?
Have you given these things to the Lord through
   prayer?

The Marriage Workout

When I am in the gym, my favorite machine is the Lifestep (think Stairsteps meets exercise cycle). The digital display shows, among other things, your amount of steps per minute. That is my rate. So I set a goal. My rate should not fall below sixty steps per minute no matter how I may feel. Some days, this is more difficult to do than others. Even though I am capable of sustaining that rate for fifteen minutes, it takes a consistent act of engaging my will to do so. Let my mind stray for just a second or listen to the demands of my body, and the rate drops down to forty steps per minute. Forty is my comfort level. It is the level at which I operate virtually unconscious. It takes no act of will, no overcoming the flesh, no drive beyond my limits to sustain this rate for fifteen minutes.

The problem is should I succumb to that, I would not reach the physical conditioning I set out to get. Unconsciously serving the Lord, men can be good husbands and women can be good wives. It is a level of service somewhere above society's standards and below God's desire for our marriages. From here, we can operate in perpetuity—no great act of will, no discernable discomfort, cruise control, or autopilot all the way.

We may feel a nagging frustration that we are not getting the benefits we could out of marriage. This is because we are not actively relying on God to sustain our level of service. Certainly, God gets the glory. He is the reason for our every breath, but do we acknowledge Him often enough? Do we exercise our faith to perform in our marriage? If not, our results are unsatisfactory.

It is only through the conscious, consistent exercise of our faith that the true potential for marriage will be reached. This means operating at a level of service as a husband, wife, mother, and father that would be impossible to sustain but for increased reliance on the One who sustains us.

The Lord has blessed my wife and me with great careers, a good income, and time to enjoy it. This, however, is not why God brought us together. There are changes that need to take place in us that can only occur when we are together. Separated, in our individual careers, we don't have the chance to influence one another. This is too often the case with most marriages, where the couple leads separate lives every day. Even the weekends are spent doing separate activities in a quest to get more done.

It is only through the conscious, consistent exercise of our faith that the true potential for marriage will be reached.

Operating like this, the couple need only keep from getting on each other's nerves to remain married, an unconscious level of service. My wife and I decided we needed to be thinking about God more consistently. This would mean giving up what has become comfortable for what God has ordained for us to do. This would first entail determining what God has ordained for us. This alone takes a greater conscious reliance on God as we commune with Him through prayer, fasting, and just being still so we can hear His voice. Then we have to prepare for things we have not planned on doing and see no way of achieving. God's vision is always greater than the vision we have for ourselves.

Now, when we get up in the morning, it's no longer just thanking God for our blessings and business as usual. It's more like saying, "God, only You can get us through this day to achieve what You would have us do. We don't see exactly how it's going to get done, but You obviously have a plan because You purposed it in our hearts. Whether we succeed or fail today, we know we are on the right path because You have set us on it."

Do you know if you are on the right path? Is God ordering your steps each and every day? Does something happen in your life every day that makes you think only God's intervention could have brought this result? Do you live each day praying to God to get you through something and then watching the results? Do you know what God has promised you? Are you living those promises?

Start building your faith with little things. Pray for the kind of job that will balance your family life and career. Pray for a better, more accommodating home for your family. Pray for a car that is safe and reliable, not just one to get you from point A to point B.

God has done all this and more for my wife and me when we did not see how it could happen. Of course it took a great deal of obedience on our part in the areas of finances, relationships, education, and behavior, but every sacrifice we made brought us closer to God. I had to learn to be a great husband, not just a good one, in order to lead my family toward our vision. We had to learn how to be happy in our marriage through the disappointments because there were many. We had to study the Scriptures to learn what exactly God's promises were and how they applied to our life. We learned to need each other more as we took on greater responsibilities to achieve our goals. I have matured in my faith through the experience of God coming through for me consistently. Now my wife and I want to come through for God by living our lives as holy sacrifices and serving God through our ministry. It's His destiny for us, and it is our obligation to Him who first gave us life and then gave it more abundantly.

Exercise your faith and your marriage benefits. Set a goal to reach a level of service that takes the active, persistent engagement of your will, a level that only God can sustain in you. As we increasingly rely on Him, He will never let us down.

One day this new level of service will become the new norm at which you operate virtually unconsciously. The process will begin again with new goals and standards, and our faith will build ever more. God wants us to strive for the potential of our marriages so we may ultimately glorify Him.

Scripture References

Proverbs 21:9
Proverbs 31
Ephesians 5:15-16

Discussion Questions

What areas of your marriage that are currently running on autopilot?

What difficult project or experience has God brought you through recently?

What goals have you set that could absolutely not be achieved without the cooperation of your spouse?

Message in a Bottle

"If my people, who are called by my name, will humble themselves and pray and seek my face and turn from their wicked ways, then will I hear from heaven and will forgive their sin and will heal their land."

2 Chronicles 7:14

Close up picture: I am curled into a ball with arms wrapped around my shins and my chin digging deep into my knees. Pan out: I am alone on a beautiful beach of white sand and crystal waters. Where are You? We used to take long walks together and discuss intimate things. I want my Friend back. You provided for all my needs, like sending me a helpmate whom I learned to love dearly. Beneath the cross, in front of onlookers, we entered covenant with You. I held her hands and promised to remain faithful, and we donned the symbols of our fidelity. I never felt more complete.

Can someone fall from grace? If so, I certainly took that plunge. Like Lot's wife, I looked back at the burning city, just a glimpse for old time's sake. That's all it took. How weak is the flesh.

The waves come crashing in ever closer. The wet sand is tugged from beneath me to reveal trinkets of life hidden just beneath the surface, and something else, an empty bottle. Desperate, I scribble a message and place it inside. It reads, "My eyes have lusted; I have indulged my flesh with acts of immorality. My pride has marooned me on this island of titillating pleasures aimed to distract. Like salt water to a thirsty man, they fail to keep the promise of their allure. Though I knew the truth, I chose the lie and in so doing broke covenant with You, leading me to this time and place alone. Were You to accept animal sacrifices, I would butcher a goat with my bare hands. If grain was what You desired, I would harvest it until my fingers bleed. Now I can only huddle here in the chill air with just my grave clothes to warm me. How can I ask You to forgive me when I cannot forgive myself? Have You forgiven me? I don't feel You near. I want my friend back."

I set the bottle adrift into the vast ocean and cling to a sliver of faith that You may come across it. Another wave and it's gone. I want my Friend back.

Off to my periphery, just beyond the dunes, a figure approaches amid the tall marsh. I shield my eyes for a better view in the midday sun but can only make out the silhouette of a woman. I know that silhouette. I used to know her intimately but now feel so estranged from her. She approaches in a sheer white linen dress with her arms and feet bare. Her steps are hesitant and her head is held so low I cannot see the tears. Had she been there all along? At last I gazed upon her face; it held so much grief, pain, and confusion. But it is what I do not see that moves me to tears — condemnation.

There will be a time for words. For now, our expressions say what's necessary. You sent her as my helpmate. I stopped taking our long walks and having intimate conversations together in favor of her. I abandoned my Friend. When she failed to replace You, I was tempted to look back for something more. The two who became one were not complete without You. But there was no condemnation.

There beside the breaking waves, she and I made love on the cool sand. We took our time, orchestrated by the rhythm of the receding sea slapping the beach in its wake. Our only thought was of pleasing the other. Through tears of joy and reconciliation, we enveloped ourselves in Your righteousness. As we held each other, my tears turned to hyssop, cleansing me of guilt and shame until at last I could see no blemish reflected in her eyes. There on the sandy shores, we made love.

You found my bottle floating in a sea of circumstances and responded in a beautiful earthen vessel of Your own. I stand facing the sea and feel the water grip my ankles. First one foot and then the other; the water rises above my waist. Finally, I shed my grave clothes and swim for a distant shore.

Scripture References

Numbers 14:9
2 Chronicles 7:14
1 Corinthians 7:5
1 Corinthians 13:8-13
Romans 8:1

Discussion Questions

What has your spouse communicated to you that you later acknowledged was a message from God?

Did you initially receive the message or did you reject it?

Has your spouse ever had to forgive you? How did it make him/her feel?

The Basic Truth

Deuteronomy 6:23 says, "But he brought us out from there to bring us in and give us the land that he promised on oath to our forefathers."

For twenty-nine years I lived in captivity. My flesh controlled my mind and my spirit yielded. I was a desert nomad pursuing every whim or doctrine that promised an oasis. Acceptance was my god, wealth was my priest, and lust was my muse.

But You had a plan to prosper me, to give me hope and a future. She heralded that future. With her big, beautiful light brown eyes and shapely figure colored in an almond complexion, she was a model of femininity. In her, I beheld Your creative power.

I proffered my reputation knowing she would have nothing to do with my character. It was enough for now. Through our courtship, I found a way out of captivity into an unfamiliar wilderness. I was torn by my desire to be holy and my addictive behaviors. Every day with her was a battle for my soul. The flaws in my character could not sustain my appealing reputation. She soon began to notice clues. But love has a way of tolerating faults.

We pressed through problems and disagreements until at last we reached the altar. There we entered a covenant with You, and our promises were no longer just to each other. The wilderness can be an over-whelming place. With neither fire nor cloud to guide me, I have only my faith. But faith is only as good as the object in which it is placed. Will it lead me to milk and honey? Will it return me in captivity to the desires of my flesh? Free will seems at times like a blessing and a curse raining down on me.

Marriage was like a coat worn inside out. It fit, but it just didn't feel right. From the beginning, You ordained I would not be alone, but I have come a long way since Eden. The wound of my missing rib had long been covered with a callous scab. I thought You were a cruel trickster to bring me someone I so desired, knowing she could never breach my strong-holds so long as I held strong to my carnality. My home was a carnival funhouse of distorted images of myself as a man, a husband, and a father.

Marriage is like a coat worn inside out. It fits, but it just doesn't feel right.

Ashamed, I lashed out at the mirrors. I hurled verbal stones with the power of life and death only to wound the ones I loved, perhaps forever. At last, I came—excruciatingly, inexorably, brokenly—to the end of myself. There I fell exhausted into Your waiting arms, and You wept over Your prodigal son.

To You Lord, who is always faithful, powerful, and merciful, I may submit with time. Don't ask me to do the same with my wife, who is fallible, lives life within the boundaries of her fears, judges discriminately, and loves conditionally. Should I give up the very freedom bequeathed me in Christ Jesus?

Then from my pastor's mouth you spoke these words: "There is no freedom without choice." My choices were to either submit to the covenant I entered with You or go my own way and remain in bondage to sin. Freedom through submission—the very thought of this paradox makes my mind spin. Though I will not pretend to understand Your grand plan, it is enough I walk by faith on the road of matrimony.

"There is no freedom without choice."

I notice something strange on my journey. I am no longer the same person I was when I started, and neither is my wife. The only person who has not changed throughout this whole journey is You. You are the same today as You were yesterday. Because You haven't changed, neither have Your promises. With my wife, I have prospered. In our marriage, I have hope and a future.

Jeremiah 29:11 says, "'For I know the plans I have for you,' declares the LORD, 'plans to prosper you and not to harm you, plans to give you hope and a future.'"

Scripture References

Deuteronomy 6: 23
Jeremiah 29: 11

Discussion Questions

How did you feel about marriage when you first got
married?

Compare this with how you feel about marriage
now.

How has your life changed for the better since getting
married?

What's in a Title?

As an IT professional, at times I make house calls to my clients who work from home. One particular client, a single woman in her forties, shared with me that her grandmother passed on just a few days ago and she was really taking it hard. She told me she went to her boyfriend's house over the weekend for solace. When she told him over the phone her grandmother passed, he was at first silent on the other end. After some time, his response was, "I don't know what to say."

This was upsetting to my client, who felt he was the one person she could go to and be comforted by during this difficult time. She wanted him to be there for her. Instead, what she experienced was a feeling of distance. During our conversation, I thought to myself, "Are people still using the term 'boyfriend' at forty?" I was married at twenty-nine, so I was really clueless. Furthermore, what did she expect from a boyfriend?

A boy is an immature form of the male species. In the context of human relationship, he is someone whose character is not ready to handle the greater complexities inherent with being in an intimate relationship with another. A friend is a person whose relationship to another is somewhat closer than an acquaintance and less then marriage. Join the two words together and the definition becomes a person close to you who is not ready for marriage. Once again, what did my client expect?

I related her situation back to my own experience in June 9, 2001. That was the day my mother died. The family all stood around the hospital bed in silent vigil. We made the choice that the life support systems were for our benefit, not for hers, and called the doctor over. With my wife at my side, I approached the hospital bed for the last time. I took her cold, lifeless hand. It felt heavy in the palm of my own. And then I was five years old again, sitting at my wooden school desk with the seat attached. My gaze alternated between the open doorway and the teacher sitting at the head of an empty classroom, save for one student with a tardy mother. We waited for her to fill that doorway, both of us anxious to go home. At the sound of footsteps in the hallway, a smile lighted across my face. I began hurriedly packing away my books. Why hadn't I done this already? In an instant, my mother was at the doorway, her work clothes disheveled from rushing to get here. That didn't concern me. She had come, as she always did, to take me away from the adult supervisors who called me strange and the children who hated me for no reason. She had come to take me home, her only son, her pride and joy, no matter what others thought. *Goodbye cruel world, until tomorrow*, I thought. With feigned coolness that fooled no one, I walked toward her outstretched hand and felt its warmth in the palm of my own.

The nursing staff slowly began to turn off the machines and the apparatus that operated nonstop for days. The breathing tube was carefully withdrawn from my mother's throat. The monitor stopped blipping with hopeful crests and troughs of activity. Instead, the steady whir and straight line gave us the truth we denied for days. At last I could release her hand. *Goodbye, Mother,* I thought. *I am sure I will see you again at the end of my journey.*

I was sitting at my kindergarten desk once again. This time my teacher was not there. I was alone, staring at the doorway in hopeful anticipation. Eventually there were footsteps, but they were different this time—more steady, no rushing. Suddenly a man appeared in the door, adorned in brilliant white. He waited for me with outstretched arms.

I asked, "Where is my mother?"

He responded, "With me."

I asked, "Will You take me to her?"

He smiled a knowing smile. "Eventually."

I got up slowly from the chair and realized my leg was caught underneath the desk, which was now too small. I was grown up again. I approach the luminescent figure, unsure, tepid, wondering where my mother was. I felt like I knew this man, but in this form He was not familiar.

I asked, "Who are You?"

He smiled once again. "Your comforter."

I entered His outstretched arms. His hug felt like a mother's, like a father's, and like a husband's all at once.

"I will take you to her," He assured me once again, "but first you have a journey to take, and I will go with you." In His arms, I left the classroom. *Goodbye cruel world,* I thought. *This time there will be no tomorrow.*

There were many tears for many days, but I came to know my wife in a new way, as a comforter. Extraordinarily, she balanced giving me my space while also staying involved, covering me during this time of extreme vulnerability. She was nurturing and empathetic after recently losing her own grandmother. She was at my side, steadfast and consistent with her role as my wife. In her, I saw Jesus. In my pain, I came to know Him.

I came to know my wife in a new way, as a comforter.

I wonder if my client had a similar experience when her grandmother died. Did she become a little girl again, longing to be held? Whose outstretched arms did she run to? The arms of Jesus or a boyfriend who did not know what to say and was ill-equipped to deal with her vulnerability?

When it comes to marriage, a title makes all the difference. Man did not give you that title; God did. When God gives you a title, He imbibes you with all the power and authority necessary to act in that capacity. When you get married, God gives you the title of husband or wife because you have greater responsibilities now. You are operating on a higher level of human relationships, reserved strictly for the covenant of marriage. This new level has enormous challenges and places great weight on your spirit to deal with them. You are no longer operating in the "I" mode. "You are now 'we'—one unit—until you die." It's like someone moved into the studio apartment that is your soul with all their luggage and furniture and asked you, "Where do I put these?"

When God gives you a title, He imbibes you with all the power and authority necessary to act in that capacity.

How do you expect a boyfriend or girlfriend to handle something like that? Yet the world places that expectation on either person in the relationship. A boyfriend is in "I" mode by the very definition. The moment you place the weight of spiritual covering upon someone in "I" mode, they become strained and conflicted. They may try to rise to the task, and many boyfriend/girlfriend relationships make a terrific effort. But they do so without the spiritual authority and power of God. How can you cover each other without the covering of God?

When Adam was by himself in the garden, he had it pretty easy. I'm sure there were challenges: coming up with new names every day, keeping the ostriches from eating all the roses, and so forth. But he had no knowledge of good and evil. All he knew was there was a tree around that he shouldn't touch. Then Eve came along, some decisions were made, and the next thing you know, he was dealing with deceit, disobedience, strife, sibling rivalry, death, and so forth. But note that he was dealing with these issues under a new title—"husband." God foresaw the creation of man, his fall, and the introduction of sin into human society. In His infinite love and wisdom, He gave us an institution with which to deal with this until Christ returns: marriage.

To be sure, such responsibilities are difficult to shoulder even with God's anointing because married people have a tendency to drift back to the boyfriend/girlfriend "I" mode in which they are used to operating. My wife and I were only married two years when my mother died. I had to fight my natural impulse to push her away and deal with it on my own. I did not want her to experience this side of me because I was ashamed of my nakedness. Yet regardless of my feelings, I had to respect her title and let her in. She did a wonderful job despite her inexperience because she was led by the Holy Spirit. Mostly she sat and listened and let me cry or pine while she stayed in the vicinity. She handled my relationships with friends and relatives when I did not want to speak. I know she wanted to do more for me, but this was all I wanted and so much more than I allowed anyone to do in the past, regardless of their station in my life. I knew I could trust my wife after this experience. She could be right by my side when I was going through something. I had a human companion in my despair.

Again I thought about what my client expected from a boyfriend. As married people, we must accept our station in life. When problems arise in our relationship, our spouse does not need a "boyfriend" or "girlfriend" acting in the selfish "I" mode of spiritual separation. Regardless of how the problem started in the first place, it exists and it challenges the marriage. We must act in our role and assume all the power and authority God gave us to handle the problem and grow in the process.

I know some problems seem insurmountable. You may feel the urge to cut and run, just shut down, or shrug your shoulders and respond, "I don't know what to say." That is the boyfriend showing himself, and he is not equipped to handle the problem in your marriage. The husband and the wife are equipped. We have a special covenant with God to never step out of our role. Honor that covenant and you will have the victory over every issue that arises.

Scripture References

Proverbs 31: 10-12
Proverbs 12: 9
John 14: 16-17
Ephesians 5: 23
1 Corinthians 11: 11

Discussion Questions

How has your spouse supported you in difficult crises?

How have difficult crises affected your relationship with Jesus?

I Promise

I promised for better or worse
Richer and for poorer,
Yet through the years
Those words crashed to the floor.

I promised before God
To have and to hold
With so much conviction!
That was before the world took its toll.

I promised in sickness,
As well as in health
Yet from unconditional Love,
I stole some for myself

My Love was fresh fallen snow,
Across an endless field;
Covering my heart
So unwilling to yield…

To the promises born of passion so unbridled,
Your heart could scarcely keep still.
It covered you like a fleece
On a summer night's chill.

There were to be rainbows and rose gardens,
A life truly blessed.
I promised to be strong in the Lord.
What happened to the spirit man behind the flesh?

Did I fail to keep my promises?
We all have broken some.
But I promise from this day forward,
The best is yet to come.

Scripture References

Galatians 3: 28
Ephesians 5: 25
Ephesians 5: 28-30
Malachi 2: 14-15

Discussion Questions

What promises in your marriage have you failed to
keep?
How has it affected your relationship?

Printed in the United States
121124LV00001B/46-171/A

9 781604 773545